First published in the United States in 1999.

Fitzhenry & Whiteside acknowledges with thanks the support of the Government of Canada through its
Book Publishing Industry Development Program in the publication of this title.

Printed in Canada.
Design by Kerry Designs

10 9 8 7 6 5 4 3 2 1

Canadian Cataloguing in Publication Data

Skrypuch, Marsha Forchuk, 1954-
The best gifts

ISBN 1-55041-391-0 (bound)   ISBN 1-55041-385-6 (pbk.)

1. Breast feeding — Juvenile fiction. I. Below, Halina. II. Title.

PS8587.K79B47 1998   jC813'.54   C98-931739-0
PZ7.S45Be 1998

Fitzhenry & Whiteside

THE BEST GIFTS

Story by Marsha Forchuk Skrypuch • Pictures by Halina Below

To Mom, Orest, and Neil – with all my love.

Without the encouragement of the following friends and family, this book would not have been possible:
Gail Winskill, Joan Hepp, Martina Boone, Nan McCarthy, Cheryl Forchuk,
Joy Noel-Weiss, and Elisabeth Sterken.

A Special thank you to my agent, Dean Cooke.
— M.F.S

For my loving mother, Anna Below
— H.B.

Illustrations are done on watercolor paper using
watercolor, watercolor pencil,
prisma color pencil and graphite pencil

When Sara was born, friends and family gathered round with smiles and lots of gifts. Her parents opened each one with joy and thanked each giver for their kindness.

hen all the visitors had left, Sara's father put the gifts away. Then he sat on the bed next to Sara and her mother, cuddling as Sara's mother opened her nightgown and drew their daughter near.

Sara was wrapped in love and a light scent of lavender as the warmth of her mother's milk swirled in her mouth and filled her tiny stomach. She fell into a happy sleep.

On her fifth birthday, friends and family gathered round with smiles and lots of gifts. Sara opened each one with joy and thanked each giver for their kindness.

ut when all the visitors had left, Sara's parents helped her put the gifts away. Then Sara's father took out a love-worn story book that he had treasured since he was little. Sara's parents took turns reading it aloud to her.

Sara was wrapped in love and warmth as the words swirled around her mind. It didn't matter so much what the story was, it was who was doing the reading. Sara fell into a happy sleep.

When Sara finished school, friends and family gathered round with smiles and lots of gifts. Sara opened each one with joy and thanked each giver for their kindness.

ut when all the visitors had left, Sara and her parents put the gifts away. Sara knew that finishing school meant that she was no longer a little girl. Her father dried a tear from her eye, and then her mother gave her a small packet of lavender.

Sara held it to her cheek. As she breathed in the familiar scent, memories of her happy childhood swirled around her heart and filled her mind, and Sara was wrapped in love and warmth. She felt sad that her childhood was over, but grateful for what she had.

After years on her own, Sara found her one true love. On their wedding day, friends and family gathered round with smiles and lots of gifts. Sara and her husband opened each one with joy and thanked each giver for their kindness.

When all the visitors had left, Sara's parents helped the newlyweds put the gifts away, and then they gave a gift of their own. It was a photo album covered with fabric from Sara's baby blanket. Sara's parents had filled it with photographs of Sara growing up, and of her new husband too, growing up with his parents.

Sara's heart was filled with love and warmth. She kissed each parent on the cheek, then leaned her head against her husband's shoulder, thankful for what she had.

Years later, Sara and her husband had a baby of their own. Friends and family gathered round with smiles and gifts for baby Sam. Sara and her husband opened each one with joy and thanked each giver for their kindness.

One by one, the visitors left. The last to leave were Sara's parents, who gave to her the love-worn story book. She knew how much they treasured it and they knew how much Sam would love it. Sara wrapped her arms around her parent's shoulders and kissed them each on the cheek. Then they left.

Sara's husband put the gifts away. Then he sat on the bed next to Sara and cuddled as she opened her nightgown and drew their son near.

Sam was wrapped in love and a light scent of lavender as the warmth of his mother's milk swirled in his mouth and filled his tiny stomach. He fell into a happy sleep.

And Sara knew, as she always had —

— that the best gifts
can never be bought.

Books for Breastfeeding Moms

Huggins, Kathleen:
The Nursing Mother's Companion: Harvard Common Press, 1995.

La Leche League International:
The Womanly Art of Breastfeeding: Plume, 1997.

Pryor, Gale:
Nursing Mother, Working Mother: Harvard Common Press, 1997.

Pryor, Gale and Karen Pryor:
Nursing Your Baby: Pocket, 1991.

Renfrew, Mary, Chloe Fisher, and Suzanne Arms:
Breastfeeding: Getting Breastfeeding Right For You: Celestial Arts, 1990.

Breast Feeding Organizations

To find a breast feeding support group near you, please call

La Leche League Canada
18C Industrial Drive, Box 29
Chesterville Ontario K0C 1H0
1-800-665-4324

La Leche League International
1400 N. Meacham Rd.
Schaumburg, IL 60173-4048
1-800-LALECHE (1-800-525-3243)
website: http://www.lalecheleague.org/

*In Canada, contact your local Public Health Unit
to speak with a public health nurse.*

For more information:

INFACT Canada
6 Trinity Square
Toronto, Ontario M5G 1B1
416-595-9819
website: http://www.infactcanada.ca/

National Alliance for Breastfeeding Advocacy (NABA)
Office of Educational Services
254 Conant Rd.
Weston, MA 02193-1756
781-893-3553
website: http://members.aol.com/marshalact/Naba/

Breastfeeding Committee for Canada
PO Box 65114
Toronto Ontario M4K 3Z2
e-mail: bfc@istar.ca

International information groups:

World Alliance for Breast Feeding Action (WABA)
website: http://bbs.elogica.com.br/waba/

The International Baby Action Network (IBFAN)
website: http://www.gn.apc.org/ibfan/

To find a lactation consultant near you:

International Lactation Consultant Association (ILCA)
4101 Lake Boone Trail, suite 201
Raleigh, NC 27607
919-787-5181
website: http://www.ilca.org

Canadian Lactation Consultant Association (CLCA)
c/o Calgary Breastfeeding Center
1616 -20A Street N.W.
Calgary, Alberta T2N 2L5
403-220-9101